Companion to the Fylde

by

R.K. Davies

Published by:

Countyvise

1 & 3 Grove Road, Rock Ferry, Birkenhead,
Merseyside. L42 3XS.

ISBN 0 907768 25 3 L000234834

Printed in En~~gland~~ by BIRKENHEAD PRESS LTD.
1 & 3 Grove Road, Rock Ferry, Birkenhead, Merseyside. L42 3XS.

D1147150

DEDICATION

To my closest Fylde connection, my wife Barbara,
without whose help
this book would not have been possible.

One of the Fylde churches, typical of the places of worship in the community for well over a thousand years. Photo: Lancashire Evening Post.

Wrea Green Village green and pond. Photo: Lancashire Evening Post.

AUTHOR'S NOTES

Like so many others my first visit to the Fylde was not an event that left a lasting impression on me. I was quite young when I was taken to the Circus at Blackpool which while being entertaining enough in its own right, the journey there was to me dull in the extreme. On reflection this was because the person who took me just drove like there was no tomorrow saying absolutely nothing of the country through which we passed.

Later when I married into a local family more time was spent in the area and I began to look around a bit. By profession I am an engineer so my curiousity is aroused when I find something that requires explanation and this enquiring mind seems to always ask questions even when travelling. If I see a village, or building, or perhaps an old railway line at some point where there is on the face of it no rational explanation, I ask why is it there?

By reading and asking questions I have found so much interest that in all cases I have been able to obtain a far greater understanding of the places visited and more enjoyment than would otherwise have been possible. Friendships have been forged which make one feel that you belong. People are always more outgoing when they know you are taking an interest in their way of life rather than just treating them as objects to look at as you pass them by.

This book does not set out to be a definitive history and as far as possible I have avoided dates. Neither is it meant to be a guide book of the Fylde for goodness knows there are enough of them most doing the job far better than I ever could. What I hope I have done is gather together on these pages some of the more interesting and lesser known historical facts that explain and connect the past with the present. Hopefully this will provide much of interest to visitors and residents alike and create a greater understanding of life in this part of Lancashire which already gives pleasure to hundreds of thousands every year.

So as not to have it considered as just a series of historical sketches that could be as dull as ditch water I have included a number of legends and local anecdotes to colour the scene as well as list one or two of the area's mysteries. In some cases I have even ventured my own opinions as to what the answers to these might have been. I hasten to add that I am no expert and if you find anything out that throws more light on it than I have, then I shall really feel that in writing this book I will have fulfilled part of its purpose which is to create interest.

The other part is to give enjoyment and extra understanding which can be one and the same thing, but this is a harder factor to quantify. Each to his own is an adage that is frequently bandied about and far be it from me to change the situation. What I hope for is that those who are seeking that little extra will find this book helpful. It sets out to be a companion to any visitor to the Fylde, it can point out many things of interest as well as provide some of the answers to the inevitable traveller's question, 'I wonder what that is?' as well as give a lead in to meaningful conversations with the folk that live there.

SYMBOLS USED ON SKETCH MAPS.

IMPORTANT RAILWAY STATION.

RAILWAY (still in use)

COURSE OF OLD RAILWAY

ROAD

MOTORWAY

CANAL

MARSHLAND

PIER

ESTUARY OR CREEK

BRIDGE

TIDAL DOCK

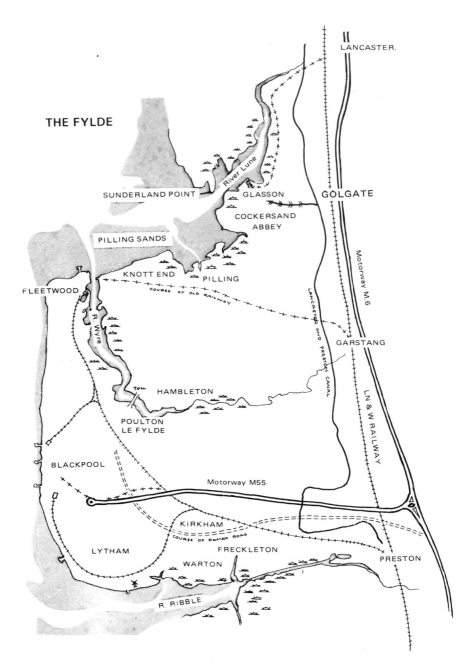

THE FYLDE

LANCASTER.

SUNDERLAND POINT
GLASSON
GOLGATE
River Lune

COCKERSAND
ABBEY

PILLING SANDS

KNOTT END
PILLING
FLEETWOOD
COURSE OF OLD RAILWAY
Motorway M.6

R. Wyre
LANCASTER AND PRESTON CANAL

GARSTANG

TOLL
HAMBLETON

POULTON
LE FYLDE
LN & W RAILWAY

BLACKPOOL
Motorway M55

KIRKHAM
COURSE OF ROMAN ROAD

LYTHAM
FRECKLETON
PRESTON
WARTON

R RIBBLE

INTRODUCTION

The Romans knew the Fylde well. Their legions marched along one of their vast network of stone paved roads which they built westwards from an encampment at Ribchester just to the east of the present day Preston. Why they did is today largely a puzzle, for one thing is certain, what they saw two thousand years ago bears no relationship to the sights and centres of population that attract hundreds of thousands along much the same route today.

The M55 carries countless cars and holidaymakers to the 'fun' town of Blackpool which didn't exist two thousand years ago, Fleetwood is a product of the last two hundred years, and Lytham, if it did exist was only a tiny fishing community hidden amongst the sand dunes. So why did the Romans want to cross the Fylde?

If we are honest there is no answer to that question, conclusions are impossible, and we can only conjecture from the few remains that have been discovered. It is a realisation of this that makes the whole area a fascinating one in which to browse. The Romans were a predictable breed, life for them followed a well defined pattern. To a very great extent their occupation of Britain was all about trade and the vast military installations they left behind served the dual purpose of being trading centres and the means of protecting them. Their undoubted realisation of the value of communications led to the building of roads which for very practical purposes were kept as straight as possible. Not only is a straight line the shortest distance between two points, but it enabled the heavy loads to be taken over the undulating countryside with the greatest ease.

This last statement requires some explanation, especially as the Fylde is one of the flatter areas on the British Isles. One can be forgiven for thinking that the easiest way of getting to the other side of a hill is to go round it, but the Romans had other ideas. Their method of getting a load over a hill was to use a system of pullies and ropes to haul it over by anchoring one end to trees or posts at each side of the road and the other end to the load itself. The rope was then pulled downhill which hauled the load up with the aid of the pulley. This method would not have been possible if the road were full of bends, so it was kept straight.

As has been observed the Romans were a race that followed a strictly defined pattern of life which gives us one of the first unanswered questions about their life on the Fylde. Their road from Ribchester follows a straight enough path all the way to Kirkham. In fact the present day high street of Kirkham is just about the same route as the Roman road. It is to the west of the town that the puzzle begins. From this point on it sweeps round to the north in a giant curve, quite out of character with the rest of their constructions. It is unfortunate that the scant remains beyond Kirkham don't tell us enough about why this almost unique feature was built in this fashion, or even where it eventually ended. The last known trace was unearthed at 'Puddle House Farm', a few miles east of Blackpool.

The last known general direction of the road would seem to indicate that it was going to finish at a point on the River Wyre somewhere to the east of the present Fleetwood. If this were so then it would more than likely have been at a fording point. I have a theory that there was probably a 'T' junction with a north to south road that connected a fording point on the Wyre with one that was known to exist on the Ribble at Freckleton a few miles south of Kirkham where the Romans were known to have had an outstation. The problem of proving the theory is that nothing is known of the exact position of the coastline or the flow of the rivers as they were two thousand years ago.

Another exciting mystery is the whereabouts of the Roman Port of 'Portus Stetenorium'. It is shown on one or two ancient maps, but its exact location is delightfully vague and no traces have been positively identified up to now. A few years ago it was thought to have been found near Fleetwood, but this was scoffed at by experienced divers who say that what was thought to have been the remains of an old quayside is in fact a natural geological feature. Local people will not have it and still lay claim to the discovery being part of the site of the Roman port.

I subscribe to the view that there was more than likely a port or landing in the district, probably at the lowest fording point on the Wyre. If this were so the direction indicated by the last known remains of the road after leaving Kirkham and turning north would point to the Wyre at or near Skippool Creek.

Because we have no real idea of the line of the coast or flow of the rivers as they were at that time all this is pure supposition. Over the centuries rivers have silted up and changed course, coastlines have extended seawards in some instances and been eroded away in others, which makes the location of many sites that no doubt did exist completely inaccessible today. All this is meat and gravy to the historian and explorers of this world, but it can be a little more than that as well. If the modern traveller has one or two of these apparently illogical facts pointed out it can give him whole new fields of interest or at least make an otherwise boring journey entertaining. As one who does much travelling, this is what history means to me and I have never found that a little curiosity does any harm Quite the opposite in fact. It has given me an insight into an otherwise strange part of our country plus many a happy hour exchanging a yarn with the good folks who live in the countryside I am passing through.

The Fylde Defined.

For our purposes the Fylde is going to be defined as the area west of the Pennines, bounded in the North by the River Lune and in the South by the River Ribble. Most will know it as the tract of flat windswept land traversed on a trip to Lytham or Blackpool. If that is all it is to you then no blame can be attached if it is considered as uninteresting, for there is little to see apart from well tended fertile fields and few places where the ground rises above fifty feet. Once one gets near the coast the Tower at Blackpool dominates the landscape and on arrival man made ammusements demand the attention of all. To believe that this is all to be had of the Fylde would be rather like coveting a car without an engine. The whole area is sprinkled with villages set like jewels on green baize surrounded by water on three sides with edges steeped in history.

As far as we know the district has been low lying and windswept for more thousands of years than are recorded in history, but we also know that it is in the last few hundred years that large tracts of the area have been drained from a marshy, hostile environment into the fertile plain it now is.

It is the edges that have attracted humans over the centuries. In the first place travel over the mosses and marshes all defiled by tidal muddy creeks was a near impossibility and the rivers and sea provided the easiest way of getting from one part to another. Today, now that the land has been drained and the rivers crossed with bridges, travel over the land is no bother. However, the latest methods of travel have brought into the district a new breed of persons. They are divided into two distinct classes, those who choose to live and make their living by the sea and those who just want to get away to the shores for a holiday. Those who live more inland are of a different stock, they are the yeoman farmers and smallholders who get their living mainly from the fertility of the drained mosses. To get off the main roads and drive along the dozens of lanes that now criss cross the Fylde is an experience in itself. These lanes are straight as a die for a few hundred yards then take sudden right angled bends. So often does this happen that to those who don't know the district the effect is thoroughly confusing and you soon loose a sense of direction. The landscape as I have said is flat giving very limited vistas. Today it is a land of isolated farmhouses and bungalows. The tallest structures are the farm silos and church towers. Frequent mists further limit visibility leaving one sure way of obtaining a sense of direction. The prevailing wind is west and to the west is nothing but flat land and sea to stop the ocean bred gales from sweeping in across to the Pennines twenty miles or more to the east. This has the effect of giving the few trees and hedges a very distinct leaning to the east.

Having recognised this you can travel in any direction for no more than ten miles and you will strike the water that surrounds the area on three sides or the mountains to the east.

Townships.

Preston and Lancaster are not truly Fylde towns although placed as they are at the south east and north east corners respectively they do serve as gateways. It is very difficult to get onto the Fylde without going through one of these two places, so it is only natural that the modern development of it is closely tied up with them. In Preston's case the railway and the docks have altered the life of Fylde dwellers to the extent that virtually the whole of the growth of Lytham, Blackpool and Fleetwood has come about in one way or another because of the growth in and around Preston. Lancaster on the other hand has long had an influence over the district because of its longer history and growth as the capital of the county. The nature of the terrain changes north of the Wyre which divides the whole district into two. Roughly one third of it lies to the north of the river and is of a more hilly character, although having said that we haven't said much because even across this northern part the highest point barely reaches one hundred feet above sea level.

It was to the south of the river that there used to be great stretches of bog with tidal creeks and streams cutting deeply into the area making travel more difficult. The result of this is that the villages and farmsteads across the northern third have been longer established and give a more traditional aspect to the countryside. The towns of Lytham, Blackpool and Fleetwood are modern creations whose present existence was brought about entirely by the development of the railways. Poulton and Kirkham are a lot more ancient, Poulton with maritime connections and Kirkham having served as the market place because of its central position.

At first glance it would seem that the whole of the Fylde is surrounded, apart from the eastern boundary, by centres of population in some way connected with the sea. This is in fact a modern concept although up to a couple of hundred years ago because of the complete lack of inland communication the vast majority of travel was coastal and by use of the waterways that riddled the area.

As we have seen the Romans it is said had a major port in the area and there is evidence of Viking settlements far upstream on the Wyre. It is therefore mainly with the marine connections that the real interest of the Fylde comes to light and while it is not my intention that this should be considered as a definitive history of the district or a guide book, it is, I hope, going to provide answers to many questions that visitors to the district will ask and perhaps even stimulate a renewed awareness for residents.

What I am going to do therefore is take each place around the Fylde Coast in turn, tell a little of its history and bring to your notice a few of the lesser known facts which will give a better understanding of what there is to be seen as well as a greater enjoyment of your surroundings.

Glasson Dock (Lancs).

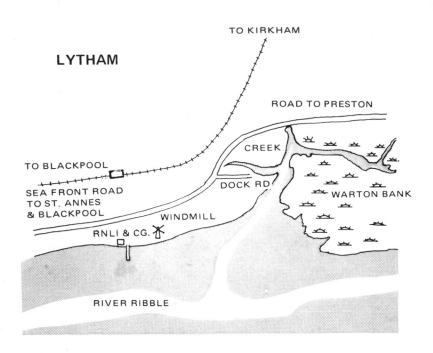

LYTHAM

TO KIRKHAM

ROAD TO PRESTON

CREEK

TO BLACKPOOL

DOCK RD.

WARTON BANK

SEA FRONT ROAD
TO ST. ANNES
& BLACKPOOL

WINDMILL

RNLI & CG.

RIVER RIBBLE

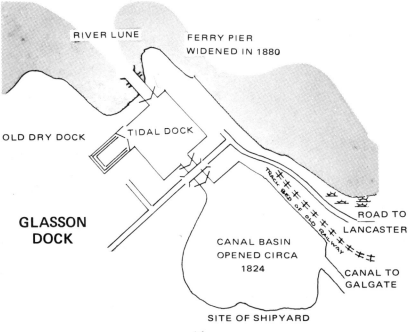

RIVER LUNE

FERRY PIER
WIDENED IN 1880

OLD DRY DOCK

TIDAL DOCK

GLASSON
DOCK

TRACK BED OF OLD RAILWAY

ROAD TO
LANCASTER

CANAL BASIN
OPENED CIRCA
1824

CANAL TO
GALGATE

SITE OF SHIPYARD

Glasson Dock, Lancs.

Sunderland Point, October 1975.

TSMV Monas Queen, Fleetwood 1978.

Old Windmill on Lytham Green.

Fylde Wanderings.

Probably the most popular way to 'do' the Fylde is by following the shore line as closely as possible. At first sight it is an unrewarding journey, but when one pauses now and again to take a second look the trip is varied and full of fascination. I well remember driving along the edge of the sands and marshes between Glasson and Pilling one Autumn afternoon and stopping to have a look at some of the seabirds that abound. The sky was clear and clear water gurgled down the deep muddy ditch left by the ebbing tide. The scene across the Lune was completely peaceful with absolutely nothing to disturb it apart from the plaintive wails of the gulls scavenging the flotsam left by the receding waters. I did have the car radio on and at that moment it was playing an old traditional piece of French folk music. It was one of a collection of songs from the Auvergne district of France called the Shepherds Song or Ballero and sung by Victoria de los Angeles. The way in which the haunting music seemed to blend perfectly with the tranquil scene before me left an indelible memory in my mind. I began to think of what it must have been like before the days of roads and railways, a line of thought which I followed up and as a result of talking about it later heard the legend of Hugh Garth.

It would seem that Hugh was a bit of a recluse, known locally as Hugh the Hermit, he built a hut at this point on the windswept edge of Cockersands. It is said he was a kindly man, well known for his generosity towards those in need and regarded as some form of oracle. These facts gave rise to many legends some of which are still told of him. One in particular tells of how when looking for a boat to take him to Ireland, he met the Devil by a dark pool. This may or may not have been taken seriously hundreds of years ago, but it does indicate that one might have expected to find boats or ships at this point. Knowing that Sunderland Point across the river on the northern bank was used as a landing about that time, it would seem reasonable that the Southern shores were used in the same way.

During the reign of King Stephen, about 1180, a hospital was built for infirm monks and lepers on the site. This was later raised to the status of an Abbey and greatly prospered. It is known that the monks built a landing stage some time in the fifteenth century so that ships could bring in cargo and passengers to the Abbey. It must be presumed that the Abbey's produce was shipped out by the same means. What is not certain is if this jetty was the first because there seems to be a little confusion about dates in such recorded history as there is. The best indication of this is that there was also a beacon erected at this point about the same time to guide ships in through the ever shifting and dangerous channels. It is claimed that this was the first light in England, but the confusion arises over the fact that if it was put up in the fifteenth century it could not have been the first as the Romans were known to have built one at Dover at the time of their occupation.

In the Abbey's heyday ships sailed from Cockersand to Ireland, but no real records were kept and it is not known if the frequency of these sailings was such that the site could in any way be considered as a port. Apart from some remains of the Abbey and Chapter House there is little to show of past activities or glory. Certainly there are no remains to show of past maritime activities except for a modern light at the entrance of the Lune known as Abbey Light. The fact is that the view across the mud and sands now is probably as near as we are likely to get to the view that those in Roman times would have had.

The whole of the Fylde has many contrasts within its confines, its shoreline of some forty miles being no exception. One of these is to be had no more than a mile or so from the point just described. The River Lune dominates the whole northern section of the district as it makes its last sweeping curves before entering the sea. A few miles downstream of Lancaster on its southern bank is Glasson with a thriving enclosed dock believed to be the oldest enclosed dock in England, a claim I can neither uphold nor deny. One thing is certain, compared with other havens of Roman origin Glasson is modern.

In 1738 a mole was constructed here to give some shelter for local fishing boats. Its use was limited by the fact that it dried out at each low tide which didn't seem to matter then as most of the real trade on the Lune was carried out through Sunderland Point across the river and nearer the mouth. By 1787 the present dock was constructed and by the turn of the present century anything up to twenty five merchant ships were seen to be berthed there at any one time. This trade plus the fact that a railway branch from Lancaster was completed in 1883 made Glasson the main port for Lancaster. Across the river Sunderland Point which had served that purpose for nearly two thousand years suddenly declined. Glasson like a blustery winter had come in like a lion. To my mind Glasson's greatest glory is to be seen from the top of the low hill that lies behind it. Across the marshes and flatlands towards Cockersand and Pilling and further across the Lune is Sunderland Point abandoned so suddenly some hundred and fifty years ago when Glasson came into prominence. Apart from the lack of any vessels there today virtually no change has been made to the village in one and a half centuries. It is about as near as one can get to a perfectly preserved medieval seaport. The road from Overton to Sunderland runs across the marshes that line the North Bank of the river for over a mile and are covered every high tide. It is this isolation for half the time that has kept Sunderland much as it was so long ago. Even on close inspection little has changed and signs of the old maritime connections are still clearly visible.

Strictly speaking Sunderland is not part of the Fylde, but the part it has played with life on the Lune and the fact that the Lune forms one boundary of our main subject gives me an excuse to include something of its history in this narrative.

First however, lets have a closer look at Glasson itself for it is not without many points of absorbing interest. It developed rapidly after the building of the dock, the first step forward being the construction of a branch from the Preston to Kendal canal which was completed in 1826. At this time Glasson claimed to be one of the most advanced ports in Britain and as the whole of the Port of Lancaster was said to be the fourth most important this claim may be believed.

The proliferation of railway connections to other points of the Lancashire coast together with difficulties of navigation on the Lune did little to carry on the development at Glasson. Even when the branch line from Lancaster was opened in 1883 it was really too late as the more modern development at Fleetwood and Heysham slowly but surely eclipsed Glasson's glory. However it didn't decline overnight as did Sunderland. A small shipbuilding and repair yard flourished and up to a couple of decades ago there was a small dry dock there. By a quirk of circumstances the canal today provides Glasson with the bulk of the reason for a continued existence. It ends in a large basin which has a lock entrance to the tidal dock and both basin and dock are usually to be seen full of pleasure craft varying from sea going motor yachts to small dinghies. The old dry dock is now filled in and has a small industrial estate on it. The Port of Lancaster office is still there and beside two or three warehouses of modern construction there is a ships' chandler which can supply the yachtsman with most of his needs.

The tidal dock has the occasional coastal vessel in with cargo to unload, but these are few and far between these days. Outside the dock itself a riverside wharf was built which seems to have had many ups and downs. For a short period in the early 1970s a container service was operated to the Isle of Man and Ireland from here, but unfortunately this was short lived. From time to time the whole of the village is dominated with an impressive, but sad sight of one of the cross channel packet steamers laid up awaiting demolition. The last one I saw was the Isle of Man Steam Packet Company's 'King Orry'. The old 'King' didn't want to go, for when the company decided to withdraw her she was towed from Liverpool to Glasson to await disposal and not only was her short trip round the coast marked with drama, but so was her stay at Glasson.

While being hauled out of her berth at Liverpool one of the towing lines snapped causing a fatality on the quayside at Liverpool. When she was finally moored alongside at Glasson tourists poured into the village to see her. It sounds melodramatic, but a few weeks after her arrival on one dark and windy night she broke away from her moorings and was blown onto a sandbank off Conder Green about a mile upstream. She was probably the largest vessel ever to enter the Lune and for the months of her stranding she stuck out like a sore thumb. At one time all hope of getting her off the sand was given up and ideas were put forward to turn her into a permanent attraction where she lay. Local initiative won out in the end and after a considerable struggle she was returned to her berth at the wharf. Considerable quantities of scrap metal were taken from her and shipped out from the tidal dock which brought a little trade to Glasson while it lasted. Eventually the hulk of the 'King Orry' was towed away to the Medway for final scrapping leaving Glasson to return to its sleepy self.

What the population of the village is I have no idea, but I would venture to suggest it would normally be about the two hundred mark. For such a tiny place it is full of interest for the casual visitor, mainly of course in summer when the three pubs do a thriving trade and the inevitable gift shop sells most of its wares. Two cafes, one of them afloat on the canal basin provide lunches and teas, while the little Post Office sells a variety of provisions and post cards. While this may make it sound like a tourist trap, it isn't so, for most of the old atmosphere remains, as such modern development as there is has been well tucked away and is quite unobtrusive.

The walls of the old inns must be steeped in seaman's talk of trade, long gone, with foreign parts. If you talk to the right people you may even hear of the Nelson connection. For what seaport could hold its head high without some story to tell of one of our most revered sailors? Needless to say nobody is prepared to swear to the truth of the story which has it that Nelson had his ship, the Elephant, brought up the river by a blind Pilot who found his way between the tortuous channels by means of the depth of water beneath his keel and the feel of the ship. On reaching Glasson he was rowed up to Ashton Hall. Why? one may ask. To meet Lady Hamilton of course! Actually there are documents that prove the existence of a blind Pilot who was said to be in great demand on very dark nights.

The modern Glasson has more than just a whiff of the past, it seems to breathe it. Even so, it is becoming more and more popular with yachtsmen in spite of its essentially tidal nature which only allows access to the open sea for a couple of hours every tide. At high tide to stand by the tiny signal station adjacent to the sea lock gate on a summer afternoon gives you a parade of small shipping as colourful as any to be seen anywhere. The old coastal trade has all but gone, but Glasson looks set to serve the sailor for some time to come and while it does will always be worth a visit.

In these days the majority of visitors will arive at Glasson by car and when they do they will more than likely park on a piece of the village's history for the car park is on the site of the old railway terminus. Impressions of the old sleepers clearly show the layout of the tracks which last saw a train in 1964. The march of time brings about many changes that are inevitable, but still mourned by many. It must have been quite a journey to puff alongside the banks of the Lune across the muddy inlets and marshes from Lancaster. For those who like to explore this type of industrial archaeology time has not yet obscured much of the old track bed which can be followed for good sections of the route.

Glasson Dock (Lancs).

Glasson Dock about 1950.   *Photo: Lancashire Evening Post.*

Glasson Dock (Lancs).

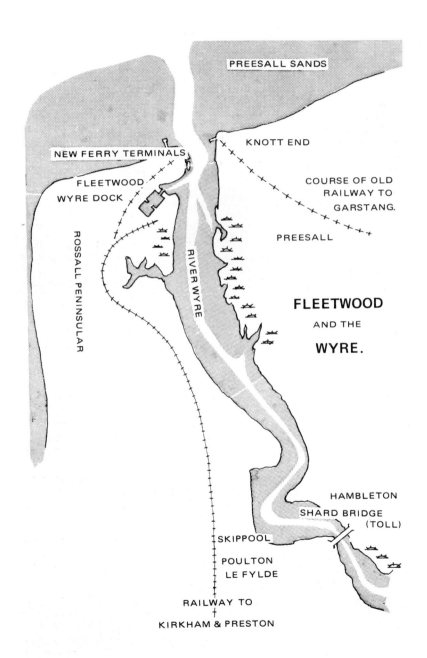

PREESALL SANDS

NEW FERRY TERMINALS

KNOTT END

FLEETWOOD
WYRE DOCK

COURSE OF OLD
RAILWAY TO
GARSTANG.

RIVER WYRE

PREESALL

ROSSALL PENINSULAR

FLEETWOOD

AND THE

WYRE.

HAMBLETON
SHARD BRIDGE
(TOLL)

SKIPPOOL

POULTON
LE FYLDE

RAILWAY TO
KIRKHAM & PRESTON

The Wyre and Fleetwood.

Only a few miles to the west as the crow flies is Fleetwood and there could hardly be a greater contrast in surroundings, atmosphere, and activities than between Glasson and Fleetwood. The whole town and everything we see in it came about one hundred and sixty years ago as a result of the aspirations of one man. He was the wealthy local landowner, Peter Hesketh Fleetwood of Rossal Hall. Rossal Hall is situated on the Rossal Peninsular between the Western Bank of the River Wyre near its mouth and the sea. He had a dream of what now would be thought of as a 'New Town' and set about creating a Packet Port with living quarters and facilities for recreation on that windswept sandy and remote corner of Lancashire.

Hesketh's ideas could never have been brought to fruition if it had not been for the advent of railways for they were centred on two concepts. The thought that this was the ideal position for a Packet Terminal to serve Ireland and that the site itself was suitable for him to create the situation where the workers could live, work and spend their leisure time in entirely separate but adjacent areas.

In pursuance of his plans he had his lands valued in the early eighteen hundreds and was informed that they were all worth £40! This sounds ridiculous until one remembers that just under two hundred years ago the Rossal Peninsular was nothing but a low sandy piece of land, no use to anybody. sticking out into the Irish Sea. Hesketh had to mortgage nearly all of his property to raise funds to get his project under way. It is said that the streets were laid out in straight lines as was intended by driving a plough through the sandy soil so that the builders would know where to put the houses. A glance at the present day map of the town shows just how successful these rather crude methods were for the dock complex and industrial sites line the western bank of the Wyre, the coastal side has now grown into a holiday resort with all the usual attractions and the centre is filled in with streets of living accommodation all laid out in straight lines.

The vital part, as well as the part that caused Hesketh his hardest work, was that a railway should be brought out westwards from Preston via Kirkham to the new town, for without it there was no chance of prosperity for it as a packet port.

Great pressure was exerted to achieve this and in 1840 the Preston and Wyre Railway was opened even before the main line was taken north from Preston to Lancaster. It terminated at what was then known as Wyre Dock which as the whole project had only been started seventeen years before, was some going. Results were proving that these machinations were not just a rich man's folly, but really were bringing many of the beneficial side effects of industrialisation to this rather remote part of the county.

Certainly the plan was taking shape, work was being brought to the river bank, houses were being built and holidaymakers were attracted to the coast where leisure time could be spent away from the industrial complex on the other side of the peninsular. The railway service was arranged to connect with the packet boats which had established regular services with Belfast, Douglas, Ardrossan and summer excursions to Piel Island off Walney. These services grew and later a very popular route to the Lakes and Furness district became established. By the mid eighteen sixties the packet boats provided the main employment for the folk of Fleetwood as the town had been named. So rapidly did this new found trade expand that in 1869 a new dock was mooted and construction started in that year.

Unfortunately funds for this major project ran short and construction was not complete until seven years later. However when it was, Fleetwood had two enclosed docks with an area totalling twenty one acres. Ships of up to two and a half thousand tons could enter the enclosed berths giving the town the biggest major boost to trade until the fishing industry became established there some few decades later. Timber, grain and considerable quantities of general cargo came to the port in addition to the packet trade and all looked set for a long period of prosperity. Unfortunately for Fleetwood, Liverpool had a determination not to be outdone which caused what should have been a period of steady growth to be one of fluctuations.

Although local fishermen had sailed from the Wyre for as long as can be remembered, it was not until the early part of the present century that it became an industry at Fleetwood. Lancashire's fisheries originally operated from Southport and Marshside south of the Ribble, but by 1900 were suffering from severe silting of the little creeks from which they sailed. The new port and town on the Wyre offered the long established fisher families a new start, so, in 1911 two families moved up the coast and in effect started the present day fishing industry that has made Fleetwood known worldwide. From these small beginnings the port became the third largest base for fishing trawlers in Great Britain.

The major part in the development of Hesketh's dream was undoubtedly played by the railway which although a separate story should not go without some brief comment. The Preston and Wyre Railway started out as a separate entity having its own ups and downs to contend with. Originally it was laid as single track from its own terminus at Preston. One of the major shareholders at the outset was John Abel Smith, a London banker, and he had also bought Roa Island near Barrow in Furness in the fond hope that he could cream off a portion of the profitable trade in minerals from the Furness area as well as develop the route from Fleetwood to Scotland. His hopes in this direction did not bear fruit quite as quickly as he had hoped due to a series of minor misfortunes which included a breaching of the embankment on which the tracks ran for the last couple of miles along the west bank of the Wyre. To prevent this happening again the line was relaid along a more westerly line to the terminus and although this got round the problem it all took time.

In 1845 and 46 two branch lines were added, one to Lytham, the other from a junction near Poulton to Blackpool (Talbot Road) which created traffic for the railway, but did nothing for Fleetwood. Twenty years later the Lancashire and Yorkshire Railway took over the line and doubled the tracks to handle the increasing traffic. The Press of the day with their usual Victorian flair reported the line as being the quickest and cheapest way to Scotland pointing out that a passenger could leave London at dawn, and be in Scotland within twenty six hours! The comment then was "What more could a man want?". It was only a year or so later when the main line was extended northwards that the same press forgot the Wyre lines and directed all their reporting skills to the new lines. Unfortunately their comments were true and the Fleetwood to Scotland packet services dwindled to nothing. Before this happened there were two minor claims to fame for the railway and the port. They were that Thomas Cook arranged the first conducted tour of Scotland via the Fleetwood lines and packet boats and a year later in 1847 Queen Victoria, Prince Albert and two of their children also used the route when returning from a cruise through the Western Isles.

In its short history Fleetwood has seen many ups and downs. The first fifty years of the present century giving a perfect example. From being a grain and cattle port with a thriving packet trade to Ireland and the Isle of Man, it grew into a major fishing port as the packet services faded away as a result of competition from the railways. Summer excursions did linger on in a desultory fashion between the wars, but never really caught on. In 1961 the last packet boat left for the Isle of Man and the railway withdrew the passenger services reducing the line to something only a little better than an elongated siding. At that time it looked as if there was only fish left which made a rather depressing picture especially as employment was becominging a major problem in the town.

They say that behind every cloud there is a silver lining and in the case of Fleetwood this would seem to have an element of truth. In spite of Cod Wars, the expense of new vessels, competition from foreign trawlers and a two hundred mile limit making the future of the fishing industry look bleak, hope that trade was about to boom in another direction turned out not to be just a pipe dream.

P & O Pandoro ferries have built a new roll on/roll off terminal just outside the enclosed dock and now operate a daily service all the year round with two large commercial vehicle ferry boats. These operate to Northern and Southern Ireland and seem to be building up an expanding business. The Isle of Man Steam Packet Company have restarted a daily trip to Douglas during the summer months from a brand new passenger terminal built a hundred yards or so downstream from the old Wyre Dock and a visit to the port at the top of the tide gives a rare close up view of marine activity.

The new ferries are impressive vessels equipped as they are with bow rudders and thrusters worming their way along the still narrow channel very close to the promenade making quite a sight for the casual onlooker. Another nice touch is that right alongside the pier head is the terminal for the last genuine tram service in Britain. Somehow they seem to give that Victorian touch that brings together the whole history of Fleetwood in one small area, the ancient and modern side by side as it were.

Just across the river a considerable amount of residential development has taken place at Knott End over the last thirty years. Most of those who live there are faced with an eighteen mile journey via the Shard Toll Bridge to get to Fleetwood, or have to use the busy little ferry across the mouth of the Wyre. All this together with a terrific expansion of the sport of sailing has brought to the river a large number of privately owned yachts which now give an air of well being to the waters of the Wyre. Taken all round there is now hope for the port, whereas two decades ago the outlook was bleak. While it isn't exactly a scene of frenzied activity all the time, the signs are that business could now build up again. The visitor is well catered for, Hesketh's dream is still as valid today as it was when first envisaged. The seaward side of the town is neat and well kept, the residential part looks matured if not exactly modern and the industrial side is rapidly rebuilding to cope with changing needs. It is a thought that the Romans built a road across the Fylde some say to give them communications with the lost port of Portus Stetenorium and now two thousand years later the M55 is doing the same thing for Fleetwood.

Fleetwood (Lancs) 1978.

King Orry awaiting breakers torch at Glasson Dock.

Fleetwood Ferry Terminal, September 1975.

Further Upstream on The Wyre.

As has been pointed out in my opening chapter the Roman influence can be detected at a number of places on the Fylde and if the road from Ribchester did reach the Wyre, then it probably did so at a point near Poulton le Fylde, a few miles upstream from the present position of Fleetwood. Of recent centuries silt has been deposited along the banks of the river and inland drainage has stopped the scouring effect of the water that previously ran off the marshy hinterland. This in turn has caused even more silt to be left behind and build up vast banks of sand off the mouth of the river. Exactly the same effect can be seen off the Ribble and off the Lune leaving the impression at low tide that the sea is a very long way a way, which it certainly is nowadays.

However, it hasn't always been like that, long before Fleetwood was ever thought of trade was carried on a considerable distance upriver. Navigation was probably quite tricky as the banks were certainly ill defined with many miles on either side being lost beneath the marshes and mud banks which were covered with water at each tide. The changes that have taken place were in many cases carried out by man, but nature also played her part. What they mean to us now is that no one can be certain of the actual course of the old river which presents us with the problem that it is impossible to know exactly where to start looking for relics of the past. The artificial banks man has built to contain the waters do not follow the course of the old river and have raised the level of the reclaimed land far above what it was centuries ago.

All this taken into consideration it is likely that the Romans did have some sort of installation near the present position of Skippool or Wardley Creek. The reason no discovery has been made to date is that whatever there was is probably now many feet under the mud that has accumulated over the last two thousand years. In this particular area there has not been the digging one associates with urban development, nor is there likely to be any in the forseeable future. So it can be said that it is not likely that there will be any accidental find from this type of activity as there has been at many other sites and we will have to wait and see if a lead will turn up that will answer so many of the mysteries that shroud the past of this corner of Lancashire.

As we have mentioned Viking influences are to be seen all over the Fylde. Their Longboats certainly penetrated some considerable distance up the River Wyre and with true Norse opportunism they settled in places just as the whim took them. Contrary to general belief these somewhat fearsome looking people didn't come with the one idea of rape and pillage in mind, although it has to be said that they probably did more than their fair share of that, they actually had trade and settlement in mind when they did come. Evidence of this abounds on the Fylde, mostly in the names of their settlements which form the basis of many of the villages of today, but also in some the long established family names which have very distinct Norse origins.

Where the Vikings went, so the Irish missionaries followed and unlike the fact that little or no trace of four hundred years of Roman occupation can be found, evidence of Viking, Irish, Saxon and even Norman influence can be seen today just about all the way from the Wyre's mouth to its source. There is little doubt that the settlements and churches started by this parade of nationalities were usually built at the limits of navigation up the numerous creeks and muddy waterways that existed at the time. As the centuries have passed and the face of the terrain has changed so these settlements have grown into the villages and townships we know today. Names of people, places and the beautiful churches being the evidence that remains for all to see.

Local fishermen have long been getting a very good living from Wyre Mussels and before the artificial river banks were built to contain the waters and prevent flooding, the whole of the river's lower reaches were flanked with sodden mosses and treacherous bogs. This tended to isolate the communities along the banks forcing them to get their living from the waters by which they dwelled.

Hambleton, long before the building of the Shard Toll Bridge, was a busy port, as were the creeks of Wardley and Skippool. Ships used to bring in Grain, Timber from the Baltic (a Viking connection at this late stage?), and many other cargoes. A Custom House was built at Poulton that still stands, its records showing that long before Glasson took trade from Lancaster and Sunderland Point, Hambleton had a major share in Lancashire's maritime business.

Once ships were built at a yard across the river from Fleetwood, a three hundred ton schooner being one of the larger ones. Warehouses lined the banks for some distance up and down stream from Poulton all helping to bring a degree of prosperity to the area which can be seen today in the atmosphere of maturity that seems to pervade the township's core. The sprawling development of modern bungalows that has spread to the very edge of Pilling Sands at Knott End has destroyed the general character of the district, but the older surviving buildings show clearly past glories. Hambleton and Poulton are full of these fascinating corners leaving us yet another opportunity to get the real feeling of yesteryear.

The creeks of Wardley and Skippool as well as the beautiful shoreline at Hambleton have become popular yachting centres, so the maritime connections to the upper reaches of the Wyre have not

Site of Old Dock at Lytham.

Sunderland Point, October 1975.

Lonely Mooring, entrance to Lytham Creek on River Ribble.

Lytham Creek Site of Old Dock.

been entirely severed by Fleetwood.

The Shard Toll Bridge provides a short cut to Pilling and Lancaster along the road which goes across the marshes lining the southern banks of the Lune back towards Conder Green and Glasson. The bus from Blackpool to Knott End uses the Shard Toll Bridge and still tolls are levied on each passenger. It used to be a penny each way and an old penny at that, alas inflation has caught up even here — many times the old sum now being demanded.

I heard a story, a wartime story, about the Shard bridge. I thought it was so typical of things that went on during those bad years and clearly tells of the good nature of Fylde folk, that it is worth telling again here.

A London born friend of mine was evacuated from the 'smoke' at the beginning of the war to get them away from the potential danger of air raids, as were tens of thousands of other children in those anxious days of 1939. It was John's luck to be sent to Blackpool, that town being considered as safe as any. Apparently it was the custom for his landlady to dole out his pocket money as sent to him by his parents in dribs and drabs. One particular Saturday he had been given his sixpence and some sandwiches and told to take himself on a bus ride. By the time he had arrived at the bus station, two valuable pence had been spent on sweets, so he asked how far he could go for two. The answer was 'Knott End lad', so he duly boarded the bus.

When they arrived at the Toll Bridge the one penny toll was taken from all the passengers including John. On arrival at Knott End he realised he hd a problem, one penny left and three needed to get him back! He must have looked pretty dejected sitting in the bus shelter wondering what to do because one of the company's staff who turned out to be the conductress on the return bus, came across and asked "What's up?". When John explained the situation that he had miscalculated the cash he would require to get back because he didn't know of the toll bridge she told him to climb aboard and sit quietly up front. John did, still wondering how he was going to pay for the journey back, never mind the toll with only one penny left. It seems there weren't too many passengers that day and the conductress was very friendly, talking to him all the way back to Blackpool. Having got him past the toll bridge and kept him happy, he looked pretty forlorn on his arrival at the bus station thinking that he was going to be asked for the full fare. The Conductress had obviously taken pity on him, for on arrival she just said "Thats all right lad, off home with you". So off he went realising that not only had he had a full day out on the bus, but had come back with a penny to spare!

He tells me he has never been back to Lancashire, but he has never forgotten the kindness of the local people, especially the unknown conductress, even now thirty five years later.

Sea Wall at Knott End with tide well up covering miles of sand, a favourite walk at low tide.
                                        Photo: Lancashire Evening Post.

Kirkham High Street before modernisation and 2000 years after Roman Chariots used it.
                                        Photo: Lancashire Evening Post.

The Seashore.

I have said that the Fylde coast is one of great contrasts and I find it strange that a town like Blackpool which influences so much of life on the Fylde today has built its reputation by virtue of being by the sea, and yet has no historical maritime connections.

Not two hundred years ago it was only a huddle of fishermen's cottages set among the sand dunes that line this part of the coast. Any shipping that had business with the Fylde or its hinterland used the Lune, Wyre or Ribble and certainly fought shy of the exposed stretch where Blackpool now stands.

The Victorian love of a promenade by the sea and getting as near to it as possible whilst maintaining decorum made the building of piers inevitable. Blackpool which fast gained a reputation for doing things on a grander scale than anyone else, built three! They are still there today, but the pleasure boats and excursion steamers have long since stopped calling. It has been said that a bus stop outside your house does not make it a bus station. By the same token Blackpool was never a seaport, so any study of ports and harbours would have lean pickings there. What has happened is the total pursuit of pleasure, there can be little doubt of that and if this is what is demanded by the public at large, then Blackpool does it exceedingly well. As I have indicated earlier this is not intended to be a guide book and in any case to list all the delights of Blackpool would fill volumes. It is historically an 'instant town' with no deep roots in the past. The trams that run along the sea front from Squires Gate in the south to Fleetwood in the north are in many ways its only piece of history. As far as I know it is the last major tram system in the United Kingdom and as such attracts thousands of visitors to the town each year. If not exactly beautiful, the views from one of these trams is a perfect one of how the British holidaymaker disports himself beside the sea.

River Wyre at Skippool Creek, this might have been site of Roman Port long since lost.

Photo: Lancashire Evening Post.

River Lune.

Lytham and the Ribble.

Somehow it doesn't seem right to gloss over Blackpool with a few short paragraphs, but as this book is meant to be a companion to anyone travelling around the Fylde it sets out to point to a few of the lesser known facts and legends connected with the district. In Blackpool's case the town's publicity department makes sure that any visitor is kept so fully informed that there is no need for me to repeat the exercise.

History begins again at Squires Gate albeit recent history for the only claim that the town has to be a port is because of the airfield that forms its southern boundary. During the second world war planes were built in the large hangars. These aircraft all helped to build up the Royal Air Force which played such a major part in winning that affray. Now the field is modernised into a busy airport with services to Ireland and the Isle of Man nearly every hour in the peak season. Hundreds of private aircraft visit the field each week and the hustle bustle of the comings and goings provides the public with an interesting sight from the well placed viewing area.

The stretch of coast with the rolling sand dunes that lies between Blackpool and Lytham St. Annes is a glimpse of what the shore must have looked like a couple of hundred years ago before the railway brought in the people that have now settled into the area. Certainly the coast between the Wyre and the Ribble was like this, but the hinterland was an entirely different kettle of fish. It was riddled with waterways that cut their paths willy nilly across the acres of moss and bog, and until man carried out drainage operations travel across the district was at best difficult and at worst dangerous or impossible. This drainage didn't take place overnight, but over the last few centuries so apart from one or two places such as Lytham itself, or Freckleton we don't really know how long the actual coastline has been where it is now.

As we have seen with the Wyre over the centuries there have been alterations to the river's course. Some of these have been because of natural causes and some by the activities of man. Whatever the cause the silting of the river itself and the build up of massive accumulations of sand at the mouth has altered the whole aspect of the shoreline. It is fairly safe to conclude that the same effect has given rise to the miles of sand that now clog the estuary of the Ribble. Recent dredging of the shipping channel upriver to Preston has influenced the situation of Lytham, in many ways affecting its development as we shall see later. In centuries gone by it could be that the Ribble had a meandering course similar to the Lune and Wyre. It does seem too good to be true that it always had the almost straight course that it has now for its last eighteen miles before entering the sea. This is actually pure surmise and if only partially true means that much of the older history lies under the mud and sand as it does with the two neighbouring rivers a few miles to the north.

We do know that Lytham got itself a mention in the Doomsday Book. Not a lot is recorded of its past except that fishermen have launched their craft from the beach for many centuries and the windmill on the Green stands on the site of a mill that existed seven hundred years ago. Apart from that we know little of the really early days.

There is rather a good opening to a booklet published by the Lytham St. Annes Civic Society written by Geoff Byron who was born and brought up in the town. It is, and I quote; "IN the beginning there was sand — sand in profusion, but there was also the sea and the sky". This has given rise to the name of "Sandgrown un" for those who like Geoff were born in Lytham.

Recent local government reorganisation has lumped Lytham and St. Annes into one administrative unit, admittedly it is difficult to tell these days when one leaves St. Annes and enters Lytham. The best line of demarcation is the modern artificial boating lake at Fairhaven. It is near enough the truth to say that west of the lake is St. Annes and east of it is Lytham.

St. Annes itself is a product of the last one hundred and fifty years, it has no real history maritime or any other. The sea front is typical, it has a pier, rows of hotels and guest houses, a wide and pleasant shopping centre backed by streets of well kept semis and bungalows. It is clearly a holiday and retirement town, but vastly different in character from its near neighbour Blackpool. The whole atmosphere of St. Annes is one of genteel relaxation and well being.

Lytham on the other hand has a far more mature atmosphere, almost village like in its aspect. In spite of this the vast part of its development from the tiny fishing community it was hundreds of years ago was brought about by the railway in exactly the same period as St. Annes. In the middle of the nineteenth century the tentacles of the railway reached Lytham bringing with it the inevitable rash of rich people from Preston and further inland wishing to set up home near the water. The Victorian houses they built behind the Green overlooking the Ribble Estuary have a basic elegance that makes them much sought after today.

Geoff Byron's opening words say just about all there is to be said about the Ribble mouth, because to this day the houses that have been built near the shore have tons of sand blown into their very front gardens. If this wasn't cleared fairly rapidly I imagine the new residents would have their frontages quickly returned to the desert like conditions that existed before they were built. It must also present special problems for them in keeping it out of the houses themselves, for blown sand seems to be able to reach places even that well known lager can't reach. I suppose the industrialists and cotton mangates who first settled there found this a small inconvenience to put up with in order to have their home in pleasant surroundings by the sea and away from the dirt and grime at their places of work.

Before the advent of the 'iron horse' the problems of inland communication that beset the Fylde equally affected Lytham. There used to be a toll road from Preston but a journey along it was both uncertain and dangerous. So, it is not surprising that Lytham had a dock of its own. Its situation at the mouth of the river made the site ideal and the trade carried out there was probably far more than has actually been recorded. There are fragments of this part of Lytham's maritime connections remaining today at Lytham Creek at the very eastern end of the town. It is roughly three miles from the Ribble's mouth and divides Lytham from the marshy wastes of Warton and Freckleton and is really the obvious place for trade to have built up. It is known that by the early eighteen hundreds that the port handled many commodities, amongst them cattle, sheep, grain, timber and even coal. There were pens for the animals and warehouses to store other goods all forming a busy little complex. In the eighteen fifties a Custom House was built at the eastern end of the Green near the site of the Windmill and an Officer in Charge was appointed who it would seem was given many duties other than collecting dues. He had to keep records of all vessels entering or leaving the port as well as acting as look out, presumably with his coastguard's hat on. Unfortunately the Custom House was pulled down, but this was not before it had seen service as an artist's studio and headquarters for the local Naval Cadets after its original purpose ceased to exist.

There is reference to the fact that one year after the railway was opened to Fleetwood a branch line was opened to Lytham from Kirkham which had its own branch some three quarters of a mile long built down to the dock. This gave access to the spreading rail network and really had the reverse effect to the one that had been hoped for. It did to a limited extent give a minor boost to the port's trade in some respects, but in others the invading rails took away more than they brought in. Today there is little to show that Lytham was once a scene of bustling maritime activity and even as I write the axe hangs over the larger port of Preston eighteen miles upstream which has as far as Lytham is concerned been the villain of the piece for nigh on the last hundred years.

When the dock at Preston was built much of the trade that up to then passed through Lytham started to use Preston with its shorter inland communications. It has to be remembered that at that time some roads were established, but except on the railways the horse was still the main means of locomotion. Rail travel was easy giving hundreds of families the chance to set up by the sea. This in turn brought with it a steady growth of trade to the town and the dock which probably would not have had such a dramatic effect on Lytham's docks fortunes had it not been for another event which was also taking place at Preston about the same time.

This other event was the building of a road bridge across the Ribble linking Preston and Penwortham. In the normal course of events this alone would have no effect whatsoever on the trade of another town, but as it happened the bridge was built across the site of a well established local shipyard belonging to Messrs Allsup who found it impossible to carry on business with their yard split in two.

They immediately started to look for an alternative site and found the declining dock at Lytham Creek to be ideal. The result of this was that in the eighteen nineties they moved their whole business down the river to Lytham Creek.

The shores of the creek provided a good place to build the vessels and launches were an easy matter. In the sixty years that were to follow over nine hundred ships were built here for service all over the world. The Lytham yard attained a justifiable reputation for real quality no matter what type of vessel it produced and these were as varied as they were many. Tugs and Ferries for rivers in Africa and South America, small passenger ships and cargo steamers plied the trade routes of the world and all left the yard with a reputation that was second to none.

The yard was also unique in another sense insomuch that they built the whole vessel, not just the hulls. The engines were built and installed in the hull after launching and the fitting out was carried out all at the same yard which I have no doubt enabled the firm to maintain a tight quality control over every stage of building which must have gone a long way to the maintaining of their high standards.

Two world wars were waged in the yard's lifetime as a shipbuilding centre and many contributions to both victories were built up this tiny creek. In the fourteen eighteen fracas a number of minelayers were built for the Royal Navy and in the second bout of hostilities between nineteen thirty nine and forty six many landing craft for our invasion forces were launched. Also connected with the invasion of the continent, large sections of the Mulberry Harbour were built and towed away from Lytham.

At its peak the yard employed over four hundred workers and life in the town must have been very good. They built so many ships that in their own way gained fame that it would be impossible to mention them all within the confines of a book such as this. For those who are interested, the booklet mentioned at the beginning of this chapter

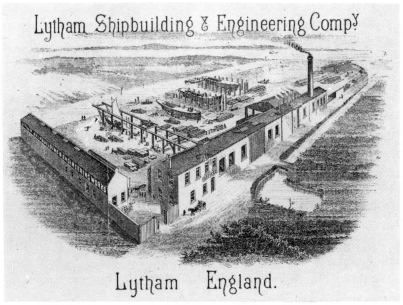

Cover of Lytham shipbuilding and Engineering Co. brochure showing their works at Lytham Creek about the turn of the century.

Late

R. SMITH & CO.

These works are now completely refitted with the newest and best machinery, and we are able to turn out the highest-class work. We make a speciality of stern wheel, twin screws, and light draft craft, orders for which we execute for shipment with the greatest possible despatch. Prices, plans, and specifications on application.

We have pleasure in handing you Illustrated Catalogue of our specialities in ship building, and shall be pleased to furnish you with tenders, plans, and specifications, whenever you are in the market.

Please Note the above change in the style of the firm. The business will be carried on by Thomas Edmundson, and Frederick Bracewell, under the name—LYTHAM SHIPBUILDING & ENGINEERING COMPANY.

How the Lytham shipbuilding and Engineering Co. represented itself.

(published by the Lytham Civic Society) goes into the subject in some depth. Geoff Byron, who wrote it, told me that he had access to enough information for a complete book on the subject of the shipyard alone. One day, when time allows, I think I will see what can be done in this direction as it would be a pity if these records are lost for all time.

Before I explain the sudden decline of what was a prospering business two of the vessels built there deserve a special mention as they bring a small piece of local history into a context that most of us, young and old, can remember. Strangely, these two were also the first and last to be built at Lytham. The first was a small steam launch called the 'Zaire'. She spent all her life on the muddy waters of an African river and sprang to fame when used in the film version of Edgar Wallace's book 'Sanders of the River' which starred Paul Robeson.

One of the last, if not the last, ships to be built by the Lytham Shipbuilding Company is one that still sails and carrys thousands of holidaymakers every year. She is the ferry that plies across Windermere, giving motorists the short route from Bowness to Coniston. It is also a strange link with this firm that the last vessel they built before leaving their Preston yard sixty years before was also a floating bridge type of ferry for the Portsmouth Floating Bridge Company, and stranger still, that also lasted until the Lytham Company stopped business before she was consigned to the scrap heap by changing circumstances.

Preston has unwittingly influenced Lytham's recent history throughout the whole of its last hundred years. We have seen how the building of the large dock took trade from Lytham's and how the road bridge across the river gave a new type of business to the town. After the second world war another of Preston's improvements was to have a dramatic effect on the estuary town. Preston was conforming to the best principals of communication by shortening the lines and bringing the means of transport as close as possible to the centre of trade by building its dock at the turn of the century. Sixty years later it had to try and keep up with changing technology. The size of shipping was increasing, especially the vessels used on the Irish Ferry Service that was building up rapidly in the nineteen fifties. The Preston Corporation did much to make the long and tricky channel better for these larger ships by dredging, rebuilding the retaining walls, and worst of all for Lytham straightening out the nasty bend in the channel just off Lytham.

As we saw on the Wyre, as soon as alterations of this nature are made to a river's course silting takes place further downstream. Unless further remedial measures are taken sand and silt build up to such an extent that the whole face of an estuary will change in a very short time indeed. In Lytham's case it was disaster, the channel to the creek became unuseable within months. The owners of the shipyard made strong representations to the Preston Corporation, pointing out that it was Preston's efforts to improve their own situation that was making life impossible at Lytham. Pleas for Preston to use their dredger to open up the channel to Lytham Creek were ignored or brushed to one side with the excuse that it would cost the Preston ratepayer too much. The arguments were long and drawn out, going on until in the end it was just not possible for shipbuilding to continue at the yard. In nineteen fifty five the company went into liquidation and the whole staff were laid off. A disaster indeed!

Now, a quarter of a century later, the creek has taken on a new lease of life. The old Dock Road has a small industrial estate and a new shipyard has come into being catering for privately owned yachts and motor cruisers. Once again a forest of masts and rigging is to be seen in the creek. The Port of Preston maintains a Pilot Station there, the cutter making a fine sight as the waters cream away from her bow as she sets off downriver to meet the container ships on their way up or down the Ribble.

Perhaps the strongest link with the past, although not all of it local, is the delightful little 'Lytham Motive Power Museum'. This has many extremely interesting exhibits including a short length of narrow gauge railway. A few years ago I paid a visit to the museum and got into conversation with a Mr. Haythornthwaite who was doing a real craftsmans job of refurbishing an old Pullman Railway Coach. Although his home was actually across the Ribble he had strong Fylde connections. He told me that his uncle was the last of the licenced river pilots for the Lune and knew more about the river than I could possibly hope to record here, but he also told me much of the connections and influence of Sunderland Point with life on the Fylde in days gone by. After listening to him I realised that even this isolated community which is strictly speaking not even on the Fylde could be said to have contributed to Lytham being what it is today. This tenuous connection is made by the surmise that according to legend the first cotton to be brought into this country was landed at Sunderland Point. In turn this virtually started the cotton industry and the mill owners were amongst the first to come and build their homes at Lytham. Far fetched? Maybe, but it does show what a tight knit community the real Fylde folk are.

The RNLI maintain a lifeboat station on the Green a couple of hundred yards from the windmill which must still be one of the best navigation marks for the Ribble. It will certainly be one of the first, and last, sights sailors see as they enter or leave the river. Alas there is no maritime commerce at Lytham now, but the connections with the sea are still very strong. In these days of change who is to say that better things are not to come?

It is ironic that as this is being written the Port of Preston has only a very short time left. The upsurge in container shipping, running to tight schedules, finds that the eighteen mile trip up the Ribble to Preston can only be made when the tide is right and is too time consuming and expensive. Much of this traffic has now been diverted to Fleetwood or Heysham and the remaining traffic has dwindled to such an extent that the days of Preston's dock are now numbered. The cost of maintaining it has escalated to such heights that the port is running at an intolerable loss to the ratepayers. Its closure will be a sad loss to Preston as it will certainly put a large number of people out of work in an area where they are suffering more than most with unemployment problems.

Lytham about 1950 view across Ribble Estuary towards Southport in background.

Photo: Lancashire Evening Post.

Site of Old Dock at Lytham.

Winter scene on beach at St. Annes.   *Photo: Lancashire Evening Post.*

Bridge over canal and rail viaduct at Old Mill Village of Galgate.
Photo: Lancashire Evening Post.

Up T'Ribble.

I started this book by telling of the Roman connections in the Fylde and carried on by retailing the various ways in which subsequent events have influenced life and environment in the district. It must have been noticed that most of the legends and stories have had a strong maritime flavour. While I have to admit to being drawn to the sea myself this treatment of the book has not been deliberately biased that way. There are two real reasons for it, the first being that by far the vast majority of visitors to the area naturally make their way to the coast and secondly that the whole areas development has come inwards from the sea.

Before I move inland as it were there are two further slices of history which will explain much of what there is to be seen today.

Looking at the map we can see that apart from being straighter than the Lune or the Wyre, the Ribble is very similar. Its banks are flanked with miles of marshy ground spreading considerable distances inland on either side. As with the other two rivers these marshes are deeply indented with deep gullies forming tiny creeks at high tide and presenting a picture of dark oozing mud forming a happy hunting ground for wild fowl at low water.

Two or three miles upstream from Lytham we come to Warton and Freckleton. Warton was, not so long ago, an area covered by thousands of acres of moss land. Now most of this has been drained and reclaimed to form the site for British Aerospace's factory and airfield. Modern jet aircraft are built and test flown from here before being sold to customers all over the world.

Freckleton which is now for all practical purposes one with Warton, was a known settlement two thousand years ago. I have mentioned that the Romans had an outpost here, probably because it was the lowest point on the Ribble that could be forded at low tide. Dredging operations of the last century have long since destroyed the ford, but at one time most of the trade from the nearby River Douglas across on the South Bank must have used this as a crossing place. There is a tiny creek that runs up to Freckleton itself which was less than two hundred years ago busy with shipping transferring cargoes to and from barges that were able to be navigated upriver to Preston. Taking into account the near primeval conditions that existed then, it is likely that because of the ford that this place was on an important north/south route from the Ribble to the Wyre.

Not unlike so many other sites with historical connections the past is buried beneath a welter of modern development. The Romans, settlers from Scandinavia, Angles, and the Normans all left their mark

51

on Freckleton, but one has to look beneath the surface of life today to find it. By this I do not mean that archaeological digs have to be carried out in everybody's back garden, for I feel there would be little to find. The evidence, such as it is, of a more subtle nature and has to be interpreted. The conditions that existed thousands of years ago are still to be seen in very small pockets along the Ribble and all over the Fylde. A good example is probably the road that we mentioned earlier that runs across the marshes near Pilling and Cockersand. The gullies and creeks that can be seen from this are much the same as those that covered many square miles each side of the Ribble's lower reaches until man took a hand in the situation.

Freckleton's straggling main street, ugly with shacks selling market garden produce, filling stations, chip shops, and a sprinkling of modern bungalows hide what was probably a very important cross roads in Lancashire's past communications. Delving into records tells us little and legends tend to mislead rather than inform, but because of the importance of any fording point or cross road, trade did build up at Freckleton, and apart from the shipping activities, connecting industries built up to support it. At one time a factory weaving sailcloth was established, some coal was imported and even a small slice of Lancashire's cotton industry was carried on in the village.

In some ways it is strange that the railways bypassed Freckleton, but the difficulties of laying the track across the bogs that surrounded the village would hardly have made any effort in this direction worth while even if it had been possible. Travelling west from Preston the modern trunk road to the coast at Blackpool has a branch off to the left that passes through Freckleton and Warton on its way to Lytham. Before the Motorway was built this road brought its own brand of misery to the inhabitants as the world and his wife became sufficiently affluent to own their own cars and caravans. The village street which formed part of the main road became so clogged that it seemed as if nothing would ever move again, especially at week ends and during the period when the famous Blackpool Lights were switched on.

Now even this road as well as the main Blackpool Road have been by passed by the M55 which has left it largely to the local traffic and the towns and villages astride them in a state of limbo. It is a far cry from the early eighteen hundreds when the old toll road was built across the thousands of acres of Freckleton Marshes, the princely sum of four old pence being paid for the privilege of being allowed to make the slow journey across.

The future of the district is difficult to see, perhaps industry and residential development will creep down the river bank to absorb these ancient townships. If it does, one hopes that the planners will be able to improve the aspect, for scant attention has been paid to beauty in these parts for the last two hundred years.

There is no need to be sad about progress, the type of heritage we have described in Warton and Freckleton should be recorded, but not I fancy all preserved. Perhaps I will be branded as a heritic for saying such things, I may even have offended a few, if this is so then I apologise, but please remember not all that was done in the past was in good taste and beauty is in the eye of the beholder. Where possible we should learn from the mistakes of the past, using newly gained knowledge to make a better future.

Blackpool Tower and Tram, August 1975.

Lighthouse, Glasson Dock.

An Outside Influence.

A glance at a physical map of the Fylde shows clearly that three of its borders are water and the fourth is formed by the Fells of the Pennines. If one then studies the population density it is perhaps not surprising that most of it is around the edges. Development of the area has been most influenced by the sea, very little coming from the inland direction except through the two gateway towns of Preston and Lancaster. I don't propose to go into the history of either of those two here as they have histories of their own which would fill volumes. However there is one place that is so unique and has influenced the whole history of the Lune. While it isn't strictly even on the Flyde, Sunderland Point is so near and has dictated the development of trade up the River, which after all forms the northern boundary of the area, that I am going to include a brief description and history of it here.

RAVENGLASS AND SUNDERLAND POINT

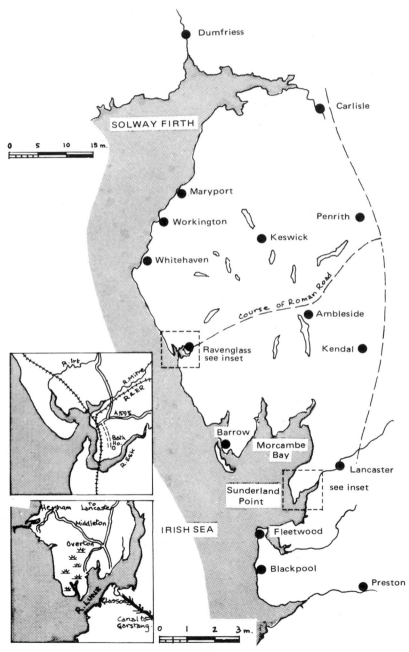

Dumfriess

Carlisle

SOLWAY FIRTH

0 5 10 15 m.

Maryport

Workington

Penrith

Keswick

Whitehaven

course of Roman Road

Ambleside

Kendal

Ravenglass
see inset

R. Irt

R.Mine
R.&.ER

A.595

Both
Ho.

R. Esck

Barrow

Morcambe
Bay

Lancaster
see inset

Sunderland
Point

IRISH SEA

To
Lancaster

Hepsham

Middleton

Overton

Fleetwood

R. LUNER

Glasson

Railway

Canal to
Garstang

Blackpool

Preston

0 1 2 3 m.

Lancashire's Lost Port.

To get the best overall view of Sunderland Point pause for a minute or two at the top of the low hill behind Glasson Dock. Look across towards the North West and you will see Sunderland on the low peninsular that protects the mouth of the Lune as it empties into Morecambe Bay. From this distance of two or three miles it all looks pretty desolate and isolated. There is little sign that less than two hundred years ago it was a major seaport bustling with ships coming and going from all parts of the world, it takes a closer inspection and a knowledge of what to look for before you can realise that up to that time it was Lancaster's lifeline and main connection with the outside world.

To reach it from the Fylde is a long journey of some twenty five miles or more and what is more it is a journey fraught with difficulties much as they were two centuries ago. The 'easy' way is to take the Morecambe Road out of Lancaster and turn off to the village of Overton which is now largely a residential centre for Lancaster, but does have fabric in its church which they claim makes it the oldest Saxon church in England. From here it is advisable to have an Ordnance Map and Tide Table for adventure starts at Overton.

The narrow road signposted to 'Sunderland' leaves Overton dropping down towards the low marshy northern banks of the Lune. Take heed of the prominent notices at each side of the road at this point for they warn that if the water has reached the foot of the posts on an incoming tide the road will be impassable and you should not proceed further. It is essential that these instructions are followed for the next mile and a quarter to Sunderland although now of Tarmac surface and marked at each side with white posts, it is in fact submerged by the sea for a few hours each side of high tide. At low tide it is often slippery and cars should take care on the stretches that have been covered by the waters as they often have flotsam and seaweed left on their surface after the waters have receded. Even in good weather the scene is a little sinister as the road winds its way through the black and oozing mud banks left uncovered at low tide. These banks are deeply cut by fast flowing and gurgling streams that drain the inland marshes which effectively cut off the peninsular from the hinterland. If your journey is being made on foot leave plenty of time as this route is cut for half of each tide period, a fact that lends all the more character to the place.

This atmosphere of isolation is the more pronounced as the only other route to the village is a long and circuitous path which is difficult to find that runs back through the dunes behind Sunderland to Middleton near Heysham. This path is only suitable for use by pedestrians and its use should only be attempted with the aid of a good map.

Don't let this picture of a seemingly grim journey put you off for once there the scene is really rewarding. On a clear day the views across the river to the Fylde shores are very pleasant, but to my mind the best one is inland with the Pennines as a backdrop running the length of the eastern horizon and the new buildings of Lancaster University set like a jewel in the mid distance. If you have brought your car, take care and park it above the high water mark just in case you have mistimed your journey and then stroll along the path beside the river in front of the two terraces of cottages to take in the atmosphere of perfect peace and 'being away from it all'.

Amongst the gathering of fishermen's cottages, now converted into beautiful private houses, were once warehouses and stores that bustled with the trade of the port. There is no great sign of decay, just a small hamlet along the river bank with well kept gardens and lawns. Some recent attempt has been made to protect the river banks from erosion and as the buildings are only set back a few feet from the river it is certain that the banks of today formed the quayside used when it was a port. Many of the old mooring stumps can still be seen now well weathered by centuries of wind and spray. Unfortunately this idyllic scene is not always to be found. Due to its exposed position the prevailing westerlies make Sunderland Point an unusually breezy place, but for the hardy ones who want a new experience the winds are worth braving and if nothing else a realisation of why it used to be called 'Cape Famine' will be gained.

The origins of this place as a port are a little indefinite although it is known that fisherfolk have operated from here for over a thousand years. I have noted that the church at Overton which was shared by Sunderland is certainly of pre Norman origin and long before it became 'discovered' the village looked to the sea for a livelihood. Fishing with 'Haaf Nets' and 'Drift Nets' was carried on from Sunderland Point by the people of Overton and to a very limited extent still is. This Haaf Net method is believed to have been introduced to these Islands by the Vikings and has only survived further north on the Solway and here on the banks of the Lune. It is practiced by the fisherman wading out as far as he can with a hand held open net and allowing the incoming tide to drive the fish towards him and into the open net. As the tide rises he wades inshore only stopping when the waters get too deep, or when he has the catch he requires.

Drift Net fishing is carried out in a different manner, a net of some two or three hundred yards long is towed out by boat and allowed to drift down river as the name implies. To this day modern versions of these ancient trades are carried on.

It is known that Lancaster was a port in Roman times, and that 'lightermen' known as Barcarorum Tigrisensum were based there. No doubt their experience gained on their native Italian river made them an ideal choice when it came to piloting the unwealdy Galleys up the tricky twisting channels of the Lune.

Another theory put forward is that they were responsible for the unloading of the Galleys into crude lighters and pulling them upriver with the tide from a point near the present position of Sunderland Point. However, I do not really consider this as likely as it was several centuries later that seagoing ships became too big to navigate as far as Lancaster. It is far more probable that these men were the forerunners of the present day pilots.

The first real record of Sunderland Point as a port comes from the 17th Century when it is known that it served Lancaster in its trade with West Africa and the West Indies. Seagoing ships used to moor to the posts that can still be seen and unload their cargoes either for storing or transfer to lighters before being taken upriver to Lancaster. Some goods were taken overland, but the quantities must have been small compared to that transported by water for the journey would have been extremely hazardous. Smaller ships certainly did sail to Lancaster, but the bulk of the trade passed through Sunderland at that time. The mooring post lowest down the estuary is still known as the Powder Stump. It was the nearest point any vessel carrying explosives was allowed to approach the port. The picture of three hundred years ago is one of hustle and bustle with a forest of masts, quite different from that to be seen today.

About the year 1700 two rows of fishermen's cottages were built by Robert Lawson, a rich Quaker merchant from Lancaster. Although now all converted these are essentially intact today and would probably still be recognised by the builder. At the peak of its trade the village also contained a rope store, joinery, Smithy and an Ale House! These are now all converted into dwellings but still retain their look of solid purpose from the outside.

One of the more frequent cargoes landed at Sunderland was hardwood from West Africa. The old Hall, one of the village's finer buildings has a mahogany staircase which probably utilised some of the timber landed literally at its front door. Cynics might think this was a seventeenth century version of 'falling off the back of a lorry' for most of the timber landed here was destined for the furniture makers of Waring & Gillow who were beginning to make a good reputation for themselves at Lancaster and later to become world famous. The Hall itself has withstood the worst the sea could do for the last three hundred years protected as it is by walls over two feet thick and a roof supported by massive axe hewn beams. Even so the river rushes in through the arched front entrance and out through the back at very high tides, it would seem that the straight through entrance forsaw this and apart from the residue left by the ebbing tide the hall is none the worse when this happens.

One of Sunderland's landmarks is the so called 'Cotton Tree', of which I shall say more later, sheltering a cottage that at one time housed a couple known locally as Bob and Lizzie. They used to take a bag of mussels, gathered locally, to the market place in Lancaster twice a week. On their return they would bring parcels back for the residents and charge one penny per package for their troubles. Now this service is carried on by a minibus from Overton, although it is doubtful if there are many bags of mussels destined for Lancaster.

In 1758 it was decided to build a weir from the Old Hall Point to the low water mark, presumably to protect the moorings. However, the Port Commissioners of Lancaster thought it would be a hazard to navigation up the Lune and ordered the work to be stopped. The next year work was once again started on this project much to the chagrin of the Commissioners who sent an enforcement officer to the village to ensure that the work was never completed. At very low tides a weir can be seen today, a little higher up the river than Old Hall Point, on the sweeping bend. This should not be confused with the one projected by the residents of Sunderland Point as it is of more recent construction. I am not sure what purpose this later weir has, but it is probably something to do with letting the natural currents prevent the approach channel to Glasson Dock from silting up.

It is said that the first cotton from America was imported into this country at Sunderland and it was a long time before anybody knew what to do with it. It is also said that seeds, from the bales stored there while people made up their minds, blew all over the village and one took root giving us what is referred to as the Cotton Tree today. I have been told that it isn't actually a Cotton Tree at all, but really a type of Black Poplar! Then there is always somebody ready to come forward and spoil a good story.

There is no doubt about it though, Sunderland's best known legend and claim to fame is the story of Sambo. It tells of Sambo, a sea captain's servant, who came here with his master and was left in the local 'Brew House' while the Captain went to Lancaster on business. Thinking his master had deserted him and frustrated by his inability to understand the language, Sambo retired to his room, refused all food and died of a broken heart within three days. In those days it was frowned upon to bury anybody who had not been baptised in consecrated ground, so Sambo was placed in a grave near the sea shore which was their way of putting his last resting place as near his homeland as possible. For the romantics amongst us this story vividly brings to life the type of simple thinking and superstition that existed at the time.

That Sambo existed there is no doubt, for the grave is there for all to see today, local children often putting flowers on it. Other stories that explain away the grave are less romantic, but probably are nearer the truth. One account tells of Sambo being seriously ill on board ship and surviving only long enough to see the mouth of the Lune. This says he died as the ship moored at Sunderland Point and was brought ashore to be buried at the water's edge.

Yet another version is that he was sick with pneumonia as the ship berthed and taken ashore to the Brew House where he could be better looked after, but died of the fever some three days later. This would seem the most likely and would explain the part of the legend that says he refused food.

Some years later Sambo's grave came to the notice of the Rev. James Watson, a retired master of Lancaster Grammar School, who had come to Sunderland Point on holiday. He wrote a seventeen verse poem about it, calling his efforts "Sambo's Elegy". This was in 1795 and the story itself must have impressed Watson because the next year he started what would be known today as day tripping. He encouraged visitors to come to Sunderland Point and collected one shilling each from them when they did. By this means he raised enough money to buy a monumental slab inset with a brass plate inscribed with the last three verses of his elegy and had it placed on Sambo's grave. This formed both a monument and epitaph to Sambo, but alas after a time weather and vandals took their toll, the inscription soon becoming illegible.

Some time later Mr. Gilchrist, a resident of Sunderland, commissioned H. Landon of Lancaster to produce a replica. When this was complete the old plate was removed and the new one put in its place where it can be seen today.

> 'Full sixty years the angry winter's wave
> Has thundering dashed this bleak and barren shore
> Since Sambo's Head laid in this lonely grave
> Lies still and ne'er will hear the turmoil more.
> Full many a sandbird chirps upon the sod
> And many a moonlight elfin round him trips
> Full many a summer's sunbeam warms the clod
> And many a teeming cloud upon him drips,
> But still he sleeps.

It is strange to reflect today on how much of the original is left for us to see, yet how little of the signs that this windswept sleepy village once bustled with activity. The quayside once lined with ships and piled high with cargoes of rum, tobacco, timber and cotton, is now deserted, left to the wind and waves. The old Look Out Station at the seaward end of the village is now converted into a cottage, but it was here that the Pilots used to wait to be hired at a cost of five shillings to guide ships up to Lancaster. Who built the villa with the Caribbean ornamental shades is a matter of conjecture. The shades and balcony might lead one to think that it was a retired merchant from the West Indies who came back to live on these bleaker shores and wanted to have just a little of the Caribbean atmosphere around him during his autumn years. It might have been that he had a Negro servant with him as this practice was not unknown up and down the Lune Valley.

Connections between Lancaster, Sunderland Point and the Slave trade were many, but slavery itself was illegal in this country and the Negro Servants that did arrive here stayed as paid servants. These were probably the lucky ones for they didn't have to suffer the miseries of bondage with their less fortunate brothers across the Atlantic, but only what for them must have been the miseries of our climate.

The building of Glasson Dock and the arrival of the railway there caused a rapid decline of Sunderland's importance as a seaport and it reverted to being a sleepy fishing community once again. Even then the rise of Fleetwood meant that the catches of the Sunderland men were landed across the waters which on a fine day gently lap the shore almost up to the walls of the two terraces of cottages. In stormy conditions storm shutters are put up and the locals rest inside their barricaded homes until the storm abates or the waters recede.

Some fishing is carried out from here today, but this is minimal and the quiet life of the village carries on unmolested by the rest of the world across the river, protected by the high tide which even controls the mighty British Post Office who has to say on the only letter box, 'collections according to tidal conditions'.

When the tide is out communication is possible with Overton and the sand, shingle and mud banks become alive with wading birds, gulls and wild life of all kinds. There is a farm protected by strong stone walls, but otherwise here is an isolated corner of Lancashire with a community totally integrated into a way of life that is governed by the tides. A deep understanding of the sea is inborn into those brought up locally and these unique conditions present no real hardships to them. It is a way of life they have no wish to change and it is essential that any visitors should respect their wishes. He would also do well to listen and heed their advice, especially concerning the tides. If he chooses to ignore it, he would not be the first to lose his car, get his feet wet, or worse still lose his life.

This is a rare community, living as it does on this sometimes beautiful, sometimes bleak corner, which has a friendly attitude towards all who are willing to stop and have a little gossip. However, one should remember that all of the land here is private and being so little of it, any damage could mean a loss of livelihood for someone. If in doubt ask, and as a bonus you could get a yarn, or a new fact or two that will be of lasting interest. The very nature of the place and its approach means that it is not equipped to deal with hoards of visitors. There are no shops or pubs on the peninsular, so should it look crowded when you arrive you would probably be doing yourself a favour by returning another day. Then there is no reason why you shouldn't be able to get the feeling of this ancient port so long lost and enjoy it to the full.

Sunderland Point, October 1975.

Sunderland Point and Mouth of Lune.

Fylde Hinterland.

To return to the Fylde proper from Sunderland Point you have to go through Lancaster. In previous chapters I have covered the coastal portions, for this is where the main interest is, but to miss out the dozens of small villages all interconnected by a maze of roads would be like eating only the outside of a soft centred chocolate, you would miss the full flavour. I do not propose to mention all of these, but rather select a few of them at random which will help to fill in the shell so far described. In the event that you become fascinated by what you read here or see on your travels then I shall have fulfilled the purpose of this book and can recommend Jessica Lofthouse's two books 'Portrait of Lancashire' and 'Lancashire Villages' as further reading.

Head south from Lancaster along the choice of routes, the railway, the motorway, or the old trunk road (the A6) and you are travelling what for practical purposes is the Fylde's eastern boundary. I find the best one is the A6 now that most of the through traffic has been siphoned off by the motorway and if you follow this route you soon come to Galgate. In the pre motorway days it was a notorious bottleneck which made motorists glad to pass, but in fact it is a real relic in microcosm of Lancashire's recent industrial past. It is astride the River Condor that finds its way into the Lune near Glasson Dock about six miles away and here beneath the railway arches is a perfect example of a cotton mill close to a long defunct tannery and ropery. The mill was closed in 1972 and such work as is to be had in the village is at the modern marina built on the banks of the Preston to Kendal canal. It is here that the so called Glasson Branch leaves the main line of the waterway to descend via six locks to sea level at Glasson. Commercial traffic has not been seen on the canal for many a decade, but the number of pleasure craft using it seems to increase every year. It is a far cry from the days before the railway when horse drawn packet boats used to provide an express service between Preston and Kendal. In passing I would mention an almost unique feature of this canal. There isn't a single lock between Preston and Carnforth, which speaks volumes for the original survey and engineering.

A few miles south of Galgate you come to the long established Fylde market town of Garstang. The bridge over the Wyre here was built by Lord Derby which helped to establish this already thriving market's prosperity. The Loyalists Earl's efforts for the town were rewarded by Charles the Second by a Charter of Incorporation being granted which gave a solid base for the trade and industries that have survived in other forms to this day. The farming communities of the Wyre Valley are still well served by Garstang, but the cottage industries that once provided the market with a roaring trade in cotton, linens, and other yarns have declined to the point where they can be considered non existent.

Sometime about the tenth or eleventh centuries the Viking longships reached the upper reach of the Wyre and as I recorded in my previous chapter on the Wyre, so the Irish missionaries followed. The Church at St. Michaels is a perfect example of where christianity was first brought to the Fylde. Even in winter when the whole district hasn't much to attract visitors St. Michaels has a rare beauty of setting and for those who take pleasure in the study of old churches this one should not be missed.

An attraction of a different sort is to be found a mile or so off the main road nearer Preston at Broughton. Here at Cuddy Hill is a pub that claims to be over five hundred years old. I couldn't find much of its history or even how long it had been a hostelry, but it certainly had atmosphere and as my visit was late in the year and at lunch time I could only praise the hospitality received.

Another Fylde village which doesn't seem to have any real historical connections but is typical of the area and quite definitely a delightful place to pause in one's travels is Wrea Green. It lies on the road between Kirkham and Lytham with its own well kept green complete with duck pond. The village Inn, The Grapes, is set back off the green opposite the pond and makes a perfect place to sit outside on a good day with your refreshment in front of you and watch the passers by.

I think that the overriding impression of the Fylde's central core today is one of rural prosperity, the villages here are not as a rule very ancient and have none of that run down unplanned look you get nearer the Ribble. Inskip just about as near the centre as you can get, is dominated by the masts of the Naval Radio Station built on the site of an old wartime airfield, but its general appearance when one gets into it is one of a neat well kept village just living its own life.

Nearby at Treales is the Derby Arms named after that well known local benefactor. The Inn itself is as well known as it is popular and is easily recognisable by the collection of motoring oddments both inside and out. On the roof is what is claimed to be the largest tyre in the world and inside the beer is drawn from petrol pumps.

Probably the main factor in the general air of neatness for the central Fylde is the fact that it is for the most part the property of the Duchy of Lancaster which of course is one and the same as saying that it is owned by the Queen. When the Coal industry was nationlised much of the compensation paid to the original owners who included the Duchy was ploughed into the development of the Fylde lands. The tenants seem a satisfied lot and proud to have the Monarch as their landlord.

The Fylde Tomorrow?

I started by saying the Romans knew the Fylde and describing Lancaster and Preston as not being of the Fylde, but gateways to it. This is true, Lancaster had its origins as a military outpost astride an important trade route and became the administrative centre for the County of Lancashire. Preston on the other hand came into being mainly as a market centre which later became industrialised. As gateways both towns have cast their influence deep in to the Fylde, along the rivers and round the coast. True as this is, I stand by my statement that neither are Fylde Towns.

Plans for a new conurbation incorporating Preston will probably creep deeper into the Fylde proper as it has already done in the south eastern corner at villages like Woodplumpton, Cottam, Broughton, Barton and Ashton. Other towns like Kirkham, Blackpool and Lytham will still have their devotees and are bound to expand. Across the river from Fleetwood there is a spread of residential property which is beginning to fill the tracts of land which at one time separated Cockersand, Pilling, Knott End and Hambleton. All these developments are attractive enough in their own way, but are quite definitely changing the character of the whole district.

Being something of a historian I tend to record the facts which on their own present a picture that is not necessarily the whole truth or true representation. For instance to say that the Fylde is a low lying, flat, windswept area bordered with marshes and sand dunes would only give half the picture. It is, or was, all of those things, but what is not said is that the low lying land having been cultivated, is green, and very fertile, studded with unspoiled villages of great beauty. To take history in isolation does not show that the development of the area from the outside inwards has now had the whole of this trend reversed by modern development. This has only really been true in the last one hundred years and an entirely new set of parameters will have to be studied before any predictions for the future can be made.

BIBLIOGRAPHY

Lancashire's Fair Face.	)	
Portrait of Lancashire.	) Jessica Lofthouse	Hayle
Lancashire Villages.	)	
AA Book of the Seaside.		Automobile Association
Return to the Lune Valley.	Stan & Freda Trott	T.W. Douglas & Son
Looking at North Lancashire.	Spartina	Dalesman
Lancashire Landmarks.	Kathleen Eyre	Dalesman
Lancaster.	Derek C. Janes	Dalesman
Lancaster.	Geoffrey Boulton	
Ports & People of Morecambe Bay.	Alan Lockett	North Lonsdale Publications
The Story of Glasson Dock.	Roger Murray	Roger Murray
West Coast Shipping.	M.K. Stammers	Shire Publications Ltd.
Railways in the North.	David Joy	Dalesman
Railways in Lancashire.	David Joy	Dalesman
Lytham St. Annes & the Sea.		Lytham St. Annes Civic Society
Inland Waterways Guide.		Inland Waterways Association
Lancashire in Colour.		Jarrold
Docks and Harbours of Britain.	Capt. A.G. Course	Ian Allan

Various articles from Lancashire Life and The Lancashire Evening Post as well as many official records have been referred to for information.

Except where otherwise acknowledged all photographs are from the author's own collection.